A CARTOON HISTORY OF THE EARTH

Volume 4: The Stick and Stone Age

Written by
Jacqui Bailey

Illustrated by
Matthew Lilly

A & C Black • London

For Joss – who's great with
sticks and stones
J. B.
For my Mum
M. L.

With thanks to
Dr Mark Collard,
of the Department of
Anthropology,
University College London.

First published in 2001 by
A & C Black (Publishers) Limited
37 Soho Square
London W1D 3QZ

Created for A & C Black
(Publishers) Limited
by Two's Company

ISBN 0 7136 5452 X hb
ISBN 0 7136 5453 8 pb

Printed in Hong Kong by
Wing King Tong Co Ltd.

As you read this book you'll see some words in bolder, blacker letters – **like this** – and some words in the hand-held panels in capital letters – **LIKE THIS**. Both types of words are listed in the Glossary on pages 30-31, where there is more information about them.

THE WORLD MUST HAVE
BEEN A QUIET, PEACEFUL
PLACE 60 MILLION YEARS AGO.
There were no giant dinosaurs
lumbering and roaring across the
land. No pterosaurs flapping and
screeching through the air, and
no monster reptiles in the sea.

In fact, there were no really LARGE animals around at all. They had all
been killed off about 5 million years earlier by a mysterious catastrophe
that changed the world's **climate**.

Now Earth's climate was hot and steamy almost everywhere, and life was getting back into action.

Lots of **species** had disappeared, but old and new types of plants and animals were rushing to fill in the gaps. ✳

✳ The MASS EXTINCTION that happened 65 million years ago killed off vast numbers of plants and animals – including all the dinosaurs. But strangely enough, some species were hardly affected at all.

Flowering shrubs and leafy ferns spread across open ground, surrounded by huge forests of oak, beech and pine trees.

YUM! LIZARD STUFFED WITH INSECT, MY FAVOURITE!

CHOMP! CHOMP! CHOMP!

Insects munched on wood or leaves, or flitted from flower to flower. Frogs and lizards fed on the insects — while snakes and birds fed on THEM!

There were lots of **warm-blooded**, furry creatures about, too. Some ate other animals. Some ate plants. A few ate anything they could get!
    The Age of **Mammals** had begun!

Some mammals became very fond of eating fish. So much so, in fact, that they took to living with them.

You wouldn't think so to look at it, but *Pakicetus* was an early type of whale. From head to tail it was only as long as a human and it still had arms and legs from the days when its ancestors lived on land.

But by about 40 million years ago, whales had lost their arms and legs and were looking a lot sleeker. They were getting BIGGER, too. *Basilosaurus* was over 20 metres long — longer than five small cars.

SWOOOSH!

Mammals took to the air, as well. *Planetotherium* was like a squirrel with a built-in parachute. It leapt from tree to tree. But pretty soon true FLYERS turned up — bats.

FLAP!

FLAP!

On the ground, new types of plant-eating mammals appeared. Now that the dinosaurs had gone there was plenty of food to go around and some **herbivores** began to grow . . . AND GROW!

Indricotherium was like a giant rhinoceros without any horns. ✱ It was about 8 metres long and 5 metres tall at the shoulder — so it could reach the leaves that other herbivores couldn't.

CHOMP!

✱ *Indricotherium* lived about 40 million years ago. It was the biggest land mammal there has ever been.

THERE, YOU SEE! EAT UP YOUR GREENS AND YOU COULD BE AS BIG AS THAT, ONE DAY.

The first elephants arrived. But these wouldn't have been much use in a circus! They were the size of a pig, with short, bendy snouts and jutting-out teeth.

The first horses were pretty small, too. *Eohippus* was just 30 centimetres high at the shoulder — about the size of a spaniel. It munched on the leaves of low-growing forest plants.

Later, it was replaced by *Mesohippus* — which was twice as big but still only the size of a greyhound.

Both were pretty fast on their feet. Which was just as well, because they were hunted by the biggest, most terrifying **carnivores** of the time — GIANT BIRDS!

A bird like *Diatryma* couldn't fly, but it didn't really need to. It was about 2 metres tall, with long, strong legs and huge clawed feet. It stalked through the forests of North America about 38 million years ago.

Giant birds weren't the only hunters, though. Meat-eating mammals lurked in the forests, including the first types of dogs and cats.

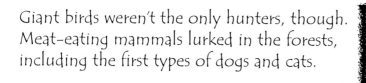

Andrewsarchus looked like a bear and a dog mixed together. It had a big heavy skull packed with strong biting teeth for chomping through plant-eaters.

GRRRR!

Cat-like *Patriofelis* was smaller, and probably used skill more than strength to catch its dinner.

AND, by 30 million years ago, a group of tree-living mammals had appeared.

They were mostly small and skinny. They ate fruit and nuts, and maybe the odd insect as well. And they were great at clinging and climbing and holding on to things.

They belonged to a larger group of mammals known as **primates**, and they were the world's first monkeys. ✱

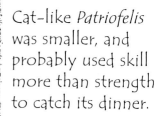

TELL YOU WHAT. YOU THROW IT TO ME AND I'LL THROW IT BACK!

✱ There are two main groups of monkeys — one group lives in South America and the other lives in Africa and Asia. One of the major differences between them is that some South American monkeys use their long tails like another arm, to move among the trees, but none of their African or Asian cousins can do this.

A few million years later, another type of primate popped up alongside the monkeys in Africa. These animals were similar to monkeys, but were usually bigger with larger brains and longer, stronger arms. They were the first APES.

C'MON GUYS, LET'S TRY ANOTHER FOREST. I'M BORED WITH HANGING AROUND HERE!

Apes loved using their long arms to swing through trees. In fact, some of them liked it so much they swung themselves right out of Africa into Asia and Europe.

So what's so special about apes?

Well, I guess if you're an owl, or an ant, apes aren't very special at all. But apes ARE special to humans because they're our closest living RELATIVES!

Scientists like to organise plant or animal species into "family" groups. The species in each group are all similar in some way, and so they are related.

To us, a wolf and a poodle may seem quite different. But to a scientist, they both belong to the group of carnivorous mammals known as "dogs".

I DON'T CARE WHAT YOU SAY, NO SELF-RESPECTING DOG WOULD BE SEEN DEAD IN THAT OUTFIT!

Apes are the animals that are most similar to us, so scientists put them into the same family group as humans. Why are they similar to us? Well . . .

SO, WHEN DID YOU START LOSING YOUR HAIR?

FIRST of all, apes and humans are both mammals. We're warm-blooded. We feed our young with milk from our own bodies. And we're covered in hair (even though human hair is sometimes hard to see).

SECONDLY, we're not just mammals — we're primate mammals. This means that we have really flexible fingers and thumbs that let us grip and hold and turn things. ✱

✱ In fact, we humans have learned to make especially good use of our thumbs. They're the reason we can paint pictures, play tennis and do up our shoelaces. Try eating your cereal one morning without using your thumb to hold the spoon and you'll see what I mean!

And THIRDLY, apes and humans are both different to other primate mammals in special ways.

We have no tail. We can move our arms around in almost every direction (a skill apes developed by using their arms to hang from tree branches), and our molars (chewing teeth) have a Y-shaped pattern on the surface.

Nowadays, there are just FIVE kinds of apes in the world — gibbons and orang-utans in Asia, and gorillas, bonobos and chimpanzees in Africa.

And there's only ONE kind of human. But once upon a time there were others — as we shall see.

NOW, WHERE WERE WE? . . . Oh, yes. By 25 million years ago, Earth's climate was changing again. The world was getting COOLER and a new group of flowering plants appeared.

These plants had flowers that were small and hard to see. The leaves were long and thin, and they grew upwards from the base of the stem.
The plants were GRASSES!

Because grass leaves sprout from the base of the stem instead of from its tip like most plants, they're quick to regrow after the stem has been cut or cropped. For plant-eaters it's a bit like having a fridge that refills itself every week!

APPARENTLY, IT'S NOT *JUST* FOR LYING ON. YOU CAN EAT IT, TOO!

What's more,
the changing climate was
tough on trees, and in some places
whole forests were dying away. They were replaced
by vast stretches of grassland. It was herbivore HEAVEN!

All sorts of animals took to grazing the grasslands. Horses were quick to give up on forest plants, and herds of them moved out into the open.

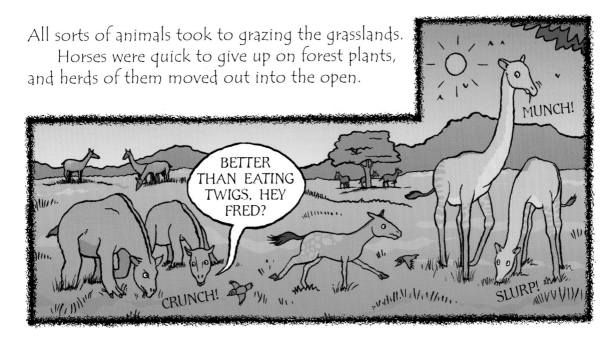

Deer, antelope, camels and giraffes soon joined them. And a mixed-up sort of creature called a chalicothere, that looked like a cross between a horse and a bear and had clawed feet instead of hooves.

With so many plant-eaters about, the grasslands were pretty good places for carnivores, too. Some of the fiercest were the cats — especially sabre-tooths. ✷

✷ Sabre-toothed cats probably used their long stabbing teeth to slash and wound their prey rather than hold on to it. Then they would simply wait for the crippled animal to die from loss of blood.

For us, though, maybe the most important grassland animals of all first appeared in Africa about 4.5 million years ago . . . they were the australopithecines.

As far as we know, the australopithecines were the first **hominids**, or human-like animals, to walk the world. * (*Australis* means "southern" in Latin, and *pithekos* is Greek for "ape".)

I KNOW YOU HATE WALKING, BUT IT'LL MAKE US FAMOUS!

* One of the oldest human FOSSILS discovered so far is a trail of footprints found in Africa. The footprints date from 3.75 million years ago. We know they were made by humans because we are the only animals ever to walk firmly upright on the soles of our feet. Scientists think these footprints were made by two australopithecines.

They were shorter than us, only about 1 to 1.5 metres tall, and their brains were smaller than ours too.

They were mainly vegetarians — although they probably ate the occasional insect or other small animal when they got the chance.

TELL YOU WHAT. YOU THROW IT TO ME AND I'LL SEE IF I CAN HIT IT WITH THIS THING!

Australopithecines must have picked up sticks and stones to poke or bash things with, just as chimpanzees do today. And it's possible that later types of australopithecine even changed the sticks or stones in some way — to make them better to use. In other words, that they MADE TOOLS.

But so far, no one's been able to prove for certain that they did.

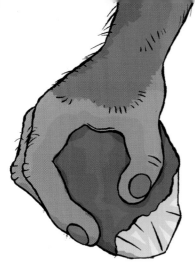

However, about 2.5 million years ago another type of human turned up in Africa — *Homo habilis*. *Homo* is the Latin word for "man", and *habilis* means "handy". It's a good name for them, because these humans definitely made tools.

The tools were very simple. Just chunks of stone that had been chipped away at the edges to make them sharp. But the difference they made was ENORMOUS.

With tools *Homo habilis* could skin an animal and chop it up for eating — an almost impossible job with just human hands and teeth.

Handy man had discovered the joy of eating regular meals of MEAT with his veg — he'd become an **omnivore**!

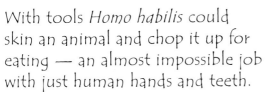

ARE YOU *SURE* THIS STUFF IS GOOD TO EAT?

But this was just the beginning. A few hundred thousand years later, yet ANOTHER type of human appeared in Africa — *Homo erectus* ("upright man"). ✷

✷ Scientists think there could have been about half a dozen different species of australopithecines, and some were still around when *Homo habilis* and *Homo erectus* appeared on the scene. For almost a million years these different types of humans shared our planet. Then, for some reason, the australopithecines and *Homo habilis* gradually died away.

As you'd expect, upright man was tall (about as tall as people are today) and strongly built, with an even bigger brain than handy man.

These people made better tools, too. And they were pretty good at hunting and gathering food. ✻

BET YOU I CAN HIT IT FROM HERE!

✻ Like *Homo habilis*, *Homo erectus* probably began eating meat by SCAVENGING the leftovers from other animals' kills. This extra food made them bigger and stronger until, using their tools as weapons, they were able to ambush and kill animals for themselves.

Even more importantly, *Homo erectus* may have been the first people to learn how to use FIRE!

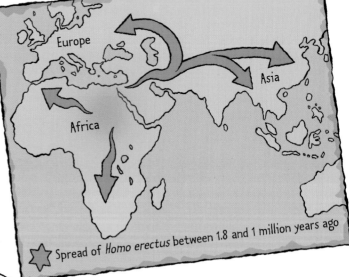

Europe

Asia

Africa

Spread of *Homo erectus* between 1.8 and 1 million years ago

DID YOU HEAR THE ONE ABOUT THE RHINOCEROS AND THE ...

A fire gave warmth, frightened away fierce **predators**, and made food a whole lot better to eat. Best of all, it was great for sitting around and hanging out with your friends.

In fact, *Homo erectus* people had so many skills they were able to go where no other hominids had ever gone before — and survive. For the first time, humans left Africa.

By 1 million years ago, *Homo erectus* people had spread to parts of Asia and were heading for Europe.

But by this time, too, the world was in the grip of a series of ICE AGES!

At times, vast sheets of ice covered the land in northern parts of the world. Along the edges of the ice sheets lay cold open plains, where only small shrubs, mosses and grass could grow, and thick forests of conifers and pines. And as the land changed, the animals that lived there had to change too.

Many died out or went south to warmer lands. But some grew thick fur coats to keep out the cold, and they learned to live with the snow and ice. There were bears and wolves, sabre-toothed cats and woolly rhinoceroses.

And there were mammoths. These huge furry elephants were more or less the same size as African elephants are today, but they were covered in a thick carpet of reddish hair and had enormous curving tusks.

TELL ME AGAIN, *WHY* DIDN'T WE GO SOUTH?

AND . . . eventually . . . people learned to live there as well.

So what are Ice Ages?

There are times in Earth's history when its climate goes through enormous changes — from hot to cold and then back to hot again.

When the climate is really cold, great ice sheets spread out from the **North and South Poles**. Much of the world's water turns to ice — the sea level falls and there is less rain. This is an ice age. ✳

✳ No one knows for certain why ice ages happen, but many scientists think it has something to do with small changes that take place in the way that the Earth travels around the Sun.

As the sea level falls, new land is uncovered around coasts. Sometimes the land forms a "bridge" that links islands and even continents.

When Earth's climate warms up again, the ice melts. The sea level rises and floods the bridges — and the lands are separated once more.

For about a million years now, the climate on Earth has been so cool that the planet is perched on the edge of freezing. Every now and then, something tips the balance and we flip into or out of an ice age. In fact, we may have had as many as TEN ice ages in the last million years.

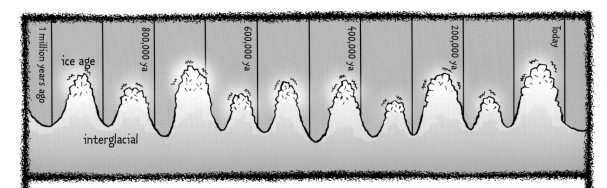

An ice age seems to happen every 100,000 years or so, with warmer periods in between. These warmer times are called "interglacials".

The LAST ice age began about 70,000 years ago. The ice spread out from the North Pole more than the South. It covered much of northern Asia, Europe and North America with ice sheets thicker than the tallest skyscraper.

A land bridge as big as a country opened up between North America and Asia. Animals used it to cross from one side to the other. They weren't the only ones. Around 15,000 years ago, humans arrived in America for the first time.

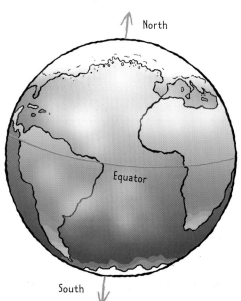

The last ice age ended around 10,000 years ago. But that may not be the end of the story. Many scientists think "interglacials" last for about 10,000 years, and that we're in one at the moment. Then the ice will RETURN.

BUT LET'S GET BACK TO OUR STORY...
By 250,000 years ago, a type of human called
Homo neanderthalensis ("Neanderthal man")
was living in Europe and the Middle East. ✱

✱ Neanderthal man
was the first ancient
human species ever to
be discovered.
    When the first
Neanderthal fossils
were found in 1856,
the bones looked so
bent and oddly shaped
no one knew what sort
of person they had
belonged to.
    People imagined
all sorts of things, but
in the end they realised
that the fossils were of
a completely different
type of human to us.

DON'T
YOU CALL *ME*
"BIG HEAD"!

Neanderthals had short, stocky bodies that were better at keeping out
the cold than tall, lanky ones. They were much stronger than we are,
with bigger heads and a bigger brain — although having a bigger
brain doesn't necessarily make someone cleverer!

WHAT
DO YOU THINK?
DOES THE
COLOUR SUIT
ME?

They lived in caves
and used fires for
cooking and for
keeping warm.
    And although
scientists haven't
found anything yet
to show that they
actually SEWED
clothes, it's likely
that they wrapped
themselves in fur
skins — taken
from the animals
they hunted.

Neanderthals have a reputation for being fierce. But they were probably quite a gentle, caring lot. They looked after family members who were too sick or too old to find food themselves.

And some scientists think they were the first humans to bury their dead. They may even have sprinkled red earth and sometimes flowers over the bodies as a sign of love or respect for the dead person.

They found a new way of making tools — by splitting a large piece of **flint** into sharp flakes that could be used as knives or scrapers.

side-scraper

AND they were fearless hunters. Neanderthals regularly went after the biggest animals on the plains. But they were often injured in the process and few lived to be more than 35 or 40 years of age (not that they were counting, of course).

But while the Neanderthals were having a tough time in Europe, ANOTHER type of human was getting ready to arrive on the scene — US! *

BYE, DEAR! HAVE A GOOD DAY AT THE HUNT.

* Our species is called *Homo sapiens* ("thinking man"). But some scientists say that we and the Neanderthals really belong to the same species. They think we both EVOLVED from different groups of *Homo erectus*. These scientists call Neanderthals *Homo sapiens neanderthalensis*, and they call us *Homo sapiens sapiens*. But to keep things simple, we'll just call ourselves "modern humans".

As far as we know, the first modern humans were living in Africa about 120,000 years ago. They were tall, probably dark-haired and dark-skinned, and their bodies were basically the same as ours are today. And we think they were our thousands-of-times great, great-grandparents!

stone knife

They were skilful tool-makers, who used fire, and hunted meat and fish and gathered plants for food. And it wasn't too long before they started to TRAVEL.

FANCY A TRIP TO SPAIN THIS SUMMER?

By about 40,000 years ago modern humans had made themselves at home in Asia and Australia, and were beginning to move into Europe.

Somewhere along the line they must have bumped into the Neanderthals. But what happened next is a MYSTERY.

Maybe we took an instant dislike to each other and started the first war.

GRRRR!

GRRRR!

WAS IT SOMETHING I SAID?

WELL I THINK SHE LOOKS JUST LIKE YOU!

Or perhaps the Neanderthals couldn't stand the sight of us and headed for the hills, where they gradually died away.

It's even possible that some Neanderthals and modern humans set up home together and began raising families. No one knows.

But however it happened, by about 30,000 years ago the Neanderthals had all VANISHED, and we were the only human species left on Earth!

carved
bone
harpoon

Strangely enough, around the time that the Neanderthals were disappearing, modern humans also seem suddenly to have become much CLEVERER!

WOW!
THIS IS MUCH
EASIER!

The tools we made were more varied than anything we or anyone else had used before.

We made spear and arrow heads and carved harpoons. We even found ways of binding the blades to wooden handles to make them easier to use.

Sometimes we lived in caves and some-times in tents made with wooden poles and animal skins.

The tents could be taken down and carried from place to place as family groups followed the herds they hunted.

IT'S SIMPLE,
BUT IT'S
HOME!

And sometimes, if people found a good place to stay for a while, they built simple houses of wood — or even of mammoth bones!

Although life was hard, it couldn't have been ALL toil and tool-making. For one thing, we began making jewellery for the first time, and decorating our clothes with shells and other stuff.

AND we invented ART! We painted pictures of animals and people on cave walls, and we carved their shapes in ivory and bone — not as tools, but as ornaments.

And although no one knows for sure, it seems likely that we'd discovered language by this time. Which meant that new ideas and ways of doing things were passed from group to group.

And, along with the ideas, we began to swop things we had made or hunted. People had discovered TRADE.

Where We Got To... When

2 By 60,000 ya, modern humans had spread to many parts of Asia. (The last *Homo erectus* people in Asia died out about 100,000 ya.)

4 Modern people moved into Europe around 40,000 ya. (The Neanderthals were already there, from 280,000 ya.)

EUROPE

ASIA

Middle East

AFRICA

1 Modern humans spread from Africa into the Middle East about 100,000 ya. ✽ (*Homo erectus* people first left Africa between 1.8 and 1.6 mya.)

Land exposed by drop in sea levels

AUSTRALIA

✽ ya stands for "years ago", and mya stands for "millions of years ago".

5,000 mya
The Sun and Solar System start to form

3,500 mya
Life begins in Earth's oceans

13,000 mya

The Big Bang

10,000 mya

The Universe Timeline

1,000 mya

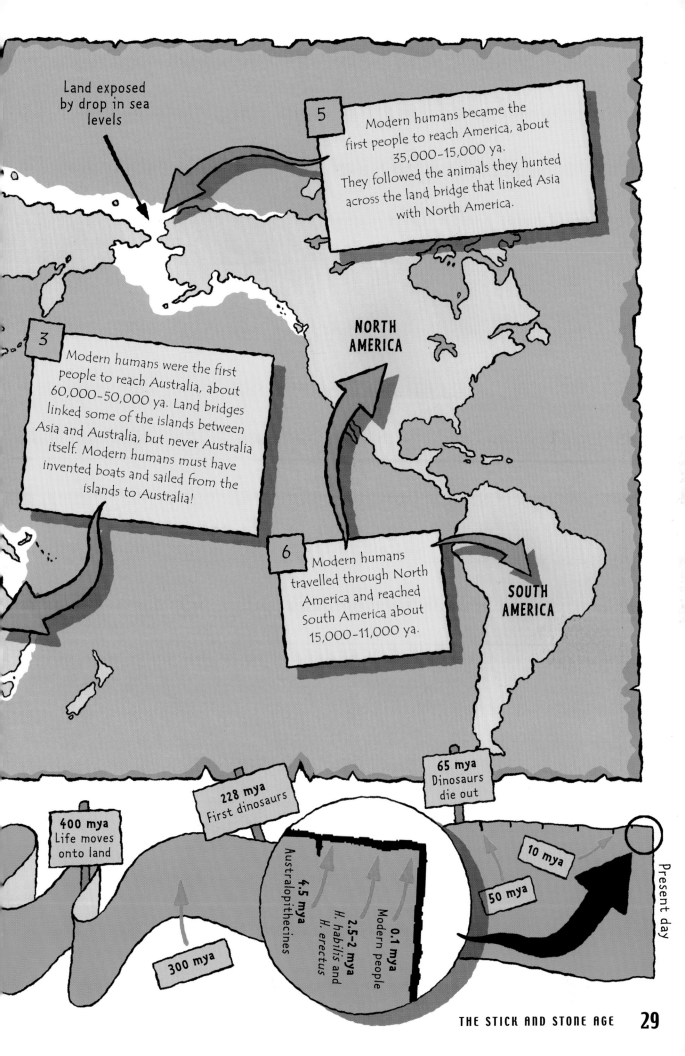

Land exposed by drop in sea levels

5 Modern humans became the first people to reach America, about 35,000–15,000 ya. They followed the animals they hunted across the land bridge that linked Asia with North America.

NORTH AMERICA

3 Modern humans were the first people to reach Australia, about 60,000–50,000 ya. Land bridges linked some of the islands between Asia and Australia, but never Australia itself. Modern humans must have invented boats and sailed from the islands to Australia!

6 Modern humans travelled through North America and reached South America about 15,000–11,000 ya.

SOUTH AMERICA

400 mya Life moves onto land

228 mya First dinosaurs

65 mya Dinosaurs die out

10 mya

50 mya

Present day

4.5 mya Australopithecines

2.5-2 mya H. habilis and H. erectus

0.1 mya Modern people

300 mya

Glossary

When you see a word here in capital letters LIKE THIS, it means that this word has a separate entry of its own where you can find more information.

carnivores The word "carnivore" means "flesh-eater". All carnivores eat other animals. Most hunt and kill their own food, but some are SCAVENGERS.

climate The pattern of weather that happens over a period of time. Weather changes from day to day, but climate changes gradually, over many years.

Usually, we talk about the climate of particular parts of the world. The climate in Iceland, for example, is colder than in most other countries, with short summers and little rain or snow.

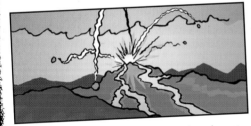

But scientists also study the climate of Earth as a whole. They've found that events such as a massive volcanic eruption can affect the world's climate. And also that over millions of years, Earth's climate has sometimes changed so dramatically it has altered the animal and plant life on this planet forever.

evolution The process by which a type of life form changes very slowly, bit by bit over millions of years, until it has become an entirely new SPECIES.

flint A hard, smooth rock often found inside other types of rock. It was used by early humans to make tools.

1. To make flint blades, the lump of flint was first chipped into an oval shape with a stone hammer.

2. Then one end was levelled off.

3. The level end was tapped with a stone hammer to break off long, thin pieces.

4. Each piece was then carefully tapped around the edges to sharpen them and shape them into the final blade.

fossils A fossil is the remains of something that lived thousands or millions of years ago. It might be part of the body of an animal or a plant, or even a group of tiny bacteria. Or it might be something an animal left behind, such as its droppings or a footprint.

Fossils have usually been turned to stone and are found buried in rock. But sometimes they are found inside amber. Amber is the hardened juice or resin produced by some trees.

herbivores Animals that feed on plants. Some SPECIES of herbivore eat a range of plants, and others eat only one type.

hominids The "family" name given to all species of human-like animals, ranging from australopithecines to modern humans. Hominids are PRIMATES that walk upright on two legs.

mammals A group of WARM-BLOODED animals with backbones and hairy skin, which produce milk to feed their young. Mammals can be divided into three kinds according to the way in which they give birth:

echidna

koala

2. Marsupials give birth to live young but they are born at a very early stage. The mothers have a special pouch on their belly and as soon as the young are born they crawl into the pouch and stay there, feeding on their mother's milk, until they are fully developed. A few marsupials live in South America, but most, such as kangaroos and koalas, live in Australia.

1. Monotremes lay eggs. There are only three species of monotreme today — an odd creature called the duck-billed platypus, and two types of echidna or spiny anteater.

cat and kittens

3. Placentals give birth to live young at a later stage, when they are more developed. Most mammals (including humans) belong to this group and they live all over the world.

mass extinctions Periods in Earth's history when large numbers of life forms die out at about the same time. No one really knows why they happen, although they are usually linked to changes in the Earth's CLIMATE. Scientists think there may have been as many as ten mass extinctions since life began.

North and South Poles If you could stick a rod exactly from top to bottom through the centre of Earth you would find that the Earth spins perfectly around it, just like a top spins on its point. This imaginary rod is called the Earth's axis, and the two ends of the rod are the North Pole and the South Pole.

omnivores Animals that feed on both plants and other animals.

predators Animals that kill and eat other animals for food.

primates A group of placental MAMMALS that includes bush-babies, lemurs, tarsiers, tree shrews, apes, monkeys and humans.

scavenging Feeding on the dead remains of other animals.

species A group of plants, animals, or other life forms of the same kind. The plants belonging to a particular species of rose, for instance, will all have flowers and leaves of the same shape and colour. With animals, the members of a species look very similar and can breed together to produce young.

Scientists are discovering new species all the time. For example, so far they've identified 980,000 different species of insect, but they believe there are many thousands more that haven't been found yet.

warm-blooded animals Can control the temperature of their bodies from inside themselves. They use food to get the energy to keep their bodies warm enough to move around. Today, only MAMMALS and birds are warm-blooded. All other animals are "cold-blooded". They use the heat of the Sun to warm their bodies, so they tend to be the same temperature as the air or water around them.

Index

Don't miss the next gripping instalments of A CARTOON HISTORY OF THE EARTH Coming soon!